Spiritual Arousal

Soulful Poetic Verses
A Journey into Connection

by
Ray Justice

Photos by Blair Hornbuckle and Deb McGwin
Cover design by Patsy Balacchi & Jill Stolt
Dandelion graphics by Jill Stolt
Management & Layout by Julie McKown

Published by Raymond Justice at Amazon.com

Copyright © 2023 Ray Justice

All rights reserved.
This book may not
be reproduced, scanned, or distributed, in whole part, or any form, printed or electronic, without written permission from the author. Thank you for not participating in any form of copying pirated materials.

ISBN: 979-8-9882172-0-6

Welcome!

You are Now
Entering the Realm of Poetic Thinking

Ray Justice's poems are the closest thing we have to Rumi's poetry in our time. That is a big statement, but to me, the truth. I don't just HIGHLY recommend; I feel his poetry is a must for any true spiritual seeker.
Michele Blood
Singer/Entertainer, Entrepreneur

This is the best poetry book I've ever read, and I say that because it felt like these incredible poems were written to me. The feeling of intimacy wraps its arms around my soul!
Laurie Sudbrink
Coach & Author of Leading with GRIT

Ray is able to make you think deeper and dream bigger than you ever imagined. His inspiring poetry will take you to places of deeper romance, curiosity, and connection with yourself. His writing is universal and will have a different effect on you each time you read it.

This book will truly exceed your expectations.
Karen Orrico
President, Creative Correspondence Centre, Inc.

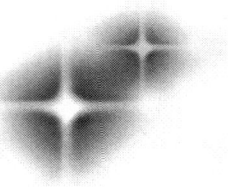

"Always wonder about the stars and why they are there."

Ray Justice

An Offer

Here
take my hand

and
step into

tomorrow

Good words about Spiritual Arousal

The first poem Ray shared with me over lunch many years ago is, to this day, still my favorite. In a crowded restaurant, I asked him to read it aloud. It spoke to me immediately, and simultaneously invited me to explore its meaning further. Ray Justice is deeply curious about the human experience in all its breadth and depth. His poetry is both intimate and universal, attuning to the wonder of human connection, in its joy and heartache, and fragility and strength.

Today working with my counseling position, the poem reflects the simplicity and complexity of relationships, what we each bring and what we long to experience. In very few words, the poem opens us to risk and vulnerability, love, and loss... our human longing to be seen, to be treated with tenderness and to be loved into our fullest selves.

p.s. The first poem he shared with me; the title is "Trust."

**~Beth Danehy, MA, MS, LMFT, CEAP
Licensed Marriage & Family Therapist**

Ray is a true master of intimacy; every word stirs the imagination. He creates poetry that invites you to energetically connect, feel, and plumb the depth of your own experience.

**~Lucia Pinizotti
MindopolyForChange.com**

Ray's poems are insightful, intuitive, and evoke a sense of spiritual mastery that will stir your soul. His deep sense of connection and curiosity for life will leave you touched, moved, and inspired.

**~Holly Geoghegan, President Golf Marketing Services
& Former Communications Director, LPGA**

Poetry is meant to evoke our feelings and emotions. Ray Justice has mastered this art with Truly fantastic poetry!

His poems are those of a Master. Unbelievable! He has created a heartfelt gift for our world to study his words because they penetrate the person. Fantastic arrangement of words.

~Donald Russell Woodruff
Author, Kangaroo Method:
How to Unlock Your Verbal Intelligence

There is something magical with Ray's writings beyond some of the stirring poetry. The language, the rhythm of some of these poems draw the reader in, and there is a corresponding sense, at a soul level, of something wonderful stirring to open the spirit. Beautiful.

~Marjorie Baker Price
CenteringTools.com

The poetry in Spiritual Arousal paints a picture with words that stimulates my sense of curiosity and wonder. Each time I read Ray's powerful writing style, I am inspired to reach deeply into my imagination for a variety of interpretations through the lens of love, friendship, nature, and family.

~Jill Stolt
CEO/Executive Director
ProsperRochester, Inc.
WellVentions, Inc.

At first, Ray's poetic verses touch your heart. Then, the poems come alive, igniting your curiosity and sense of wonder. It's like looking at your reflection on the surface of a still, smooth pond. Long-forgotten emotions begin to awaken deep within you. And you hear your soul whisper, "I'm here for you."

~Sandy Evenson, Women's Empowerment Coach &
Author of "The Woo Woo Way"
SandyEvenson.com

Table of Contents

Foreword—x

Introduction—xiv

Chapter 1: Wondering, The Beauty of Curiosity— pg 1

Chapter 2: Whispers of Intimacy, Tuning In — pg 61

Chapter 3: Arms of Oneness, Connection & Unity—pg 117

Closing Thoughts —pg 185

Dedications—pg 187

Acknowledgments—pg 191

About the Author—pg 197

Testimonials About Ray Justice—pg 203

Definitions—pg 209

A Parting Message—pg 213

Note to Myself—pg 217

Foreword

Poetry flows through Ray Justice like a stream gently trickling down the mountain. I remember Ray, and I met for coffee when he shared his notebook with several poems. With my hands wrapped around a hot cup of tea, he read each one aloud slowly and intentionally. I found myself softening my breath as I connected his words to my own personal journey.

I keenly remember the way Ray offered others the deepest part of his being, in hopes of them seeing their own light. He would sit with another so closely and create a safe and loving space with no judgment. I imagine that in that space, a person would unwrap a part of themselves with such vulnerability that it would both surprise and nurture them.

I recall the many ways he had encouraged and supported me while I was finding my way. I learned about non-judgment, a habit I had formed growing up and one I continue to work on and gaining much ground through his own example of how he problem-solved life's situations. Ray showed me the ability to view one problem from many different angles. The power of giving freely is something that I do effortlessly with no ties, and this, too, I learned from Ray.

He had always believed his one-on-one conversation was his strength; he recognized poetry was a gift that didn't come from thought but rather flowed through him and onto the paper.

I am forever grateful that Ray so intimately shared his experience and words of poetry with me that day.

One favorite is "Hands." I've read this poem many times. While the words are unpretentious, the message is powerful and has transported me from the touch of my granddaughter's tiny hand to my mom's light pat, and to the sensation of a hand in support.

"Your hands laced with mine; I feel connected."

Ray's poetry can wake us up and soothe our hearts. Like a veil lifted, it reflects a softer side, a simple point, and flawless execution.

While life is all about the journey, it's only today that we know for sure — a lesson we have learned from the past few years. Nothing is for certain; I hope you enjoy Spiritual Arousal and allow it to gently pull you into a space to breathe.

~Wendy Brabon, Dublin Ireland

Search for your
inner smile

we will know
when you find it.

One of my
favorite thoughts

is

...Hmmm!

Introduction

Let me offer you something unexpected that hits home, stirs your curiosity, and feels like it's you.

Spiritual Arousal is an educational adventure that ignites curiosity, sparks intuition, and fosters harmony. Grace, intimacy, and appreciation may awaken in the stillness of your heart as you read. Confidence grows as you allow the verses to help you feel safe exploring ideas of unity, inclusion, and community.

The intention is to create poetry that you relate to and feel, giving you the experience of energy while arousing your imagination. Please note that spaces in many of the verses indicate a longer pause, inviting you to linger and take time to ponder. Relax and let the words become part of who you are.

You're encouraged to read the Spiritual Arousal poems two or more times. The first reading gives you the words and theme. You will pick up a more profound thought or meaning when you reread it. Explore and write about the verses that get your attention. You may be amazed at what shows up as you write about these poems or others. Your journal containing poetic insights becomes a gift to your soul.

Reading in a quiet environment makes the verses more enjoyable. For instance, sit near a window to gaze outward with your thoughts. What is interesting? Write about it, just for you.

Read slowly or with a varied cadence and different pitches. When reading aloud or in my mind, I soften my voice, sometimes to a whisper, often on the last line. Many verses have a Message Phrase or Power Line, suitable for a second read and a pondering moment. In chapter one, the poem *Thoughts at Night* is an example with the sentence: **The night seems to change my thoughts.**

Everything starts with a relationship between two things. Be curious about those two things and the energy between them that is either attracting, repelling, or neutral. Spiritual Arousal poetry leads us to ponder, not necessarily to answer or decide, simply to contemplate. New windows open as we become curious and begin to wonder.

Poetry is often more profound than our basic day-to-day thinking. It's an energetic state, often stronger emotion as we know it, and becomes an aid in searching for what is driving our life.

Spiritual Arousal poetry is about that connection and relationship, creating an atmosphere and environment for Oneness. Poetry brings us deeper communication and connection beyond our regular conversations.

In the title, Spiritual Arousal, the word Spiritual represents an understanding of something bigger than us—the energy and vibration of consciousness, connections, and creativity.

Arousal is the energy of awakening excitement and the connection to all it brings. This vibrational energy then influences and arouses the Spiritual.

Intimacy's magical power is often associated with sexual relationships, yet it is also so much more and beyond. Intimacy involves connection, closeness, and how intimate we feel about ourselves and others.

Safety and a feeling of freedom are essential. Sharing with another helps build trust and intimacy. Listening to another enhances that closeness.

Understanding each other leads to openness and intimate connection.

Soulful and intimacy are words we use to describe feelings of Spiritual closeness. Listening enhances a deeper openness to understanding yourself and others.

The term Whispers, in these writings, stands for the silent, intuitive thoughts, senses, and knowing that we have in our unspoken internal awareness.

When we were young, we blew on Dandelion seeds to make a wish. Here is a modern-day version of that.

The Dandelion images in this book of Spiritual Arousals represent a whisper, a thought, or a silent Awareness. The Dandelion seeds on the cover and scattered through this book are reminders to stop and listen to your whispered insights. As you quiet your mind, you become more aware of your inner intuitive messenger.

Dandelions are pretty impressive for a little weed.

Our awareness and understandings of ourselves and others are essential to life. An ability to energetically sense and feel what is happening becomes increasingly important.

Enjoy and consider contemplating the quote on this book's back cover.

> "Always wonder about the
> stars and why they are there."

Be curious and write to yourself about it.

Are your interests aroused in Dandelions and Whispers?

You can find more information at the end of this book, where you'll also find the Closing Thoughts, Dedications, Acknowledgments, About the Author, and Definitions sections, as well as a Parting Message.

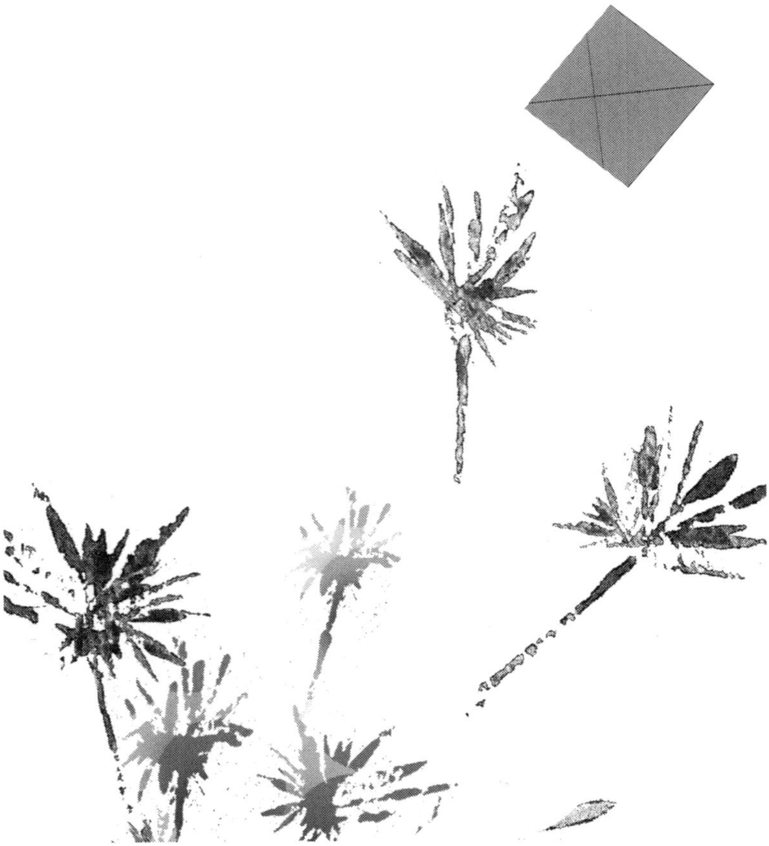

1

Wondering

The Beauty of Curiosity

Today's Intention: to have never-ending curiosity.

This first chapter, Wondering, is focused on our personal confidence and curiosities—along with our doubts, uncertainties, and disappointments—that have us wondering what is or what will be.

We often automatically label, criticize, and judge situations, people, and ways of life, before we have taken a moment to pause, wonder, and review.

Decisions are always showing up. What choices to make, which way to go, should I or should I not?

Each day set an Intention to be Curious about what shows up in your world.

Curiosity is The initial Magic, the Beginning of Imagination & Creativity. One Moment, One Insight, at a Time.

Pause, Breathe, & Be Curious
Start with curiosity and wondering about everything, it's a first step toward deeper awareness.

My Mind Wanders - My Heart Wonders

Awareness of our questions, curiosities, and wonders is a beginning step toward understanding connection and personal confidence.

Wondering about yourself while being comfortable with who you are is part of the beginning.

Intimate Connections - first with self, then with others.

I Want

I want to ask
you a question,
but I am afraid.

I need to know
the answer
before I ask.

So, I don't

      and now

           I want...

Stars

Being under
the night sky,
connecting
with the stars,

is that like
making love?

What passes
between us
you, me
    and
the heavens?

    and
which is which?

Becoming

Is it possible
> you are already

>> What you will

>>> Become?

Do I Dare?

How do I get to know you?
Am I sure? Can I trust you?

Do I dare
let you know the real me?

I need to feel safe
more certain with you.

Your smile is friendly
You are very attractive

I am more than interested
and still sit with doubt

What will show up later?

Do I dare?
      Do I dare?

           Do I dare?

If You Dream?

I wonder
if you dream of me,
at night,
when you are away from what you do.

I wonder
if you smile,
in your dreams
while we dance,
while we hold hands

I wonder
if you dream of me

or

if I am dreaming
you do.

Morning

Morning stillness

Morning calm

Waking
Peaceful

Yet ready
to begin

Today,

will I be

    the Morning?

June 17th

Before me I have three candles
on my left a smooth white one
reminds me of your purity,
your realness, your brilliance!

To my right—a red candle
symbolizing your energy,
passion and hunger.

And in the center candle
the flame burns deep
down inside,
not melting the wax away.

Your depth contained,
yet spread by a soft gentle glow.

Three flames that I feel your presence

Are there more?
Will I know them?

I am wondering,

just wondering.

June 20th

Today I lit another candle for you
It is earthy green,
    the same as
        a hundred years ago.

An old Soul
wise and knowing,

ancient in depth
    and wisdom.

July 14th

I sit
thinking of you,

as I light the nine,
mostly white
candles in front of me.

How many lives have you had before?

How many have we shared?

August 24th

Today a single candle,
a single flame,
the many aspects of you
all in one.

In this single moment
I can feel a sense
of reverence, peace
and love.

You are here
helping me

to remember.

Celebrate

What is
The music, the beat,
The song?

I know the sound,
if only I could hear it playing.

I know it's already there,
celebrating
for me

After things have turned
around
after I have made it.

This is my triumph

if I can feel it
now.

Wondering

I am wondering
where you are.
Once I am ready
will you appear?

I have been looking.
Wondering what you are like
how you will be.

Wondering, what we will
explore together.

Will you be the one
to hold my hand
pull me up
and
walk with me?

I want to search and inspire,
discover and share.

I am wondering where you are
and wonder
if you
are wondering too?

Moments

Let's sit for a spell.

What similar moments
from our past
can we connect?

What different moments
can we unite?

Each moment
as its own

yet part of another.

What?

What

will
I see

from
where

You are?

Still

Are you still
with me?

Will you
step into
my circle,

my space

and
be still

with me?

Steps

My first step
is to get past
the fear
    of you
        saying no.

My second step
is inviting you along.

Then the third step
    is loving
        each moment

when you do.

Share

I love to share
who I am,
what I see,
what I know.

And then,

you give me
another insight
    of
my unknown self.

I see further, deeper,
More
for me
to share
what I see

who I am
now

and then...

Portrait

Paint me a picture
of who you are
a portrait in words.

Describe how you see
the you that you are
and
the you
that you dream to be.

What do you feel?
Where are you Scared
and where are you Brave?

Paint for me
the depth of you.
The colors beneath
the layers,

after you have finished
the image,

the portrait
of you

will be crystal clear
and powerful.

The Space Of Poetry

I want to share
my poetry
with you.
I want to share
who I am
right now.

Then I wonder,
how do we move
into the space of a poem?

The space where we can
safely,
hear it,
feel it,
and finally
be it.

How to be the poetry
so it is part of me,
part of you,
and all
of us?

The Same

It's not about
right or wrong
this or that.

It's not about either/or.

It's about joining,
combining
the differences
while
sharing diversities.

This...

this is how creation works.

Where are we being the same?

Where are we not being creative?

Whispers

The chatter
>of my mind,

the whispers
>of my heart.

Which has the questions

that will find me?

A Thought

Was that a thought

    I just had,

a Memory?

Or one
    of your

Magical Whispers?

Are You?

I saw you
    today
or was it
    yesterday?

Are you there?
Are you real?
or
are you

my yearning?

Out Of My Mind

When I feel excited
in love
ready for fun
I can't get it out of my mind

When I feel afraid
lost
uncertain
I can't get it out of my mind

So I wonder
what is in there
in my mind
between
the love and the fear

between the confidence
and the uncertainty
that space in between
where
I stay wondering

which way will it take me
tonight

when I am alone
without you?

How Will I Know

I fell asleep
    Where are you?

Where did you go?
    What am I missing?

Will you be back?
    How will I know?

I want to wake up
    but I am afraid

Please come back and help me

Now

would be good

If Water Could Talk

They say that water
carries with it
a memory of its journey

We have to wonder
memory of what?

Is it what was touched,
felt or collected with its
continuous travels
through our world?

Water
moves along the surface,
then mixing with our clouds
up above and below
deep down under with
our rocks and soil

Always returning refreshed
while mixing and connecting
along the way

I wonder if water could tell us its story
what would we know?

... or maybe, it has been,
and we have not yet learned

its language

Electrifying Shoes

Tonight, I am wondering
where you are
what you are doing

I can sense you
and am thinking
about where you could be
and whose life you
are now enriching

You do it everywhere you go
to everyone you meet
to all of us
you make it feel better
all beautiful, special, and vibrant

You walk in electrifying shoes
we follow in your steps

We desperately try to pick up
what you have, and
to be as you are
We sort of know we can
we sense it

Yet there always seems to be
something missing, some small piece
a light bulb that needs to go off
It is there but
not quite clear.

Thank you for keeping us
wondering and stretching
while still being
in our own shoes.

A Cup Of Coffee

Years ago
Shepherds
while minding their flocks
would stop and be still
holding their staff
and gazing
at the night sky
full of stars
and their mysteries

Wondering
    what this is
        all about

Today, I watched
a woman sitting
holding a cup of coffee
feeling its warmth
being still
gazing and contemplating

what this is
    all about

We need you.

We need you
to help us
understand,
feel connected

and,
to remind us,
who we truly are.

About Tomorrow

As you prepare for your sleep tonight,
I wonder.

In that stage where you are closing your eyes,
with your thoughts of the day
and its busy to-do's.

I am curious, as you drift off,
to this world of slumber,
I am curious as to
what you will be wondering.

Your wonder,
will it flow and merge with your dreams?

And will it become
part of your nighttime reality?

This wonder,
will you remember it tomorrow,
or forever,
or not at all?

I wonder about
your wondering

The Pen And I

The pen lies silently on the paper
waiting to be of use

I also wait
wondering what to write

Both of us
Waiting... 'til later

Then the pen calls out
in its silent way

Not quite sure why
I make the choice
and pick it up

With pen in hand
my thoughts cease
as it starts to move

A connection is formed

We dance

Together
we create
a masterpiece

Heartfelt Flower

The heartfelt flower

of contemplation

It is beautiful

It is silent
while sitting
in quiet knowing

wondering
when we will share
with the world

the reflections from
our own heart

Will it be now?

My Wish

I went to the well
to make a wish

A desire
to feel safe

to feel free
to not be alone

I opened my eyes
realizing you

were already
with me

My wish

granted
before I asked...

I Have It All

All inside of me

> the peace
> the wondering
> the yearning
> the quiet
> the love
> the fun
> the fear
> the dark
> the loneliness
> the connection
> the possibilities

I have it all
except you

to share it with

Both Together

You have a smile

    that lights up the room
maybe the whole universe

you also have a finger
    that points in blame

The smile that
    grabs my heart

The finger
    that suggests
I am wrong

Both are you
    Both I feel

wonderful
    and insecure
both at the same time

both together

Yay!

Sigh!

The Table

We were all

sitting around
the dinner table

We came together
to connect
to remember each other
and who we are

But everyone
is talking
at the same time

So much noise
and confusion
who do we listen to
and who not?

We share our food
We don't share listening,
or our deeper interests

We don't share what
we are afraid of
or what brings us alive

We don't share
who
we really are

How do we learn
to understand?

How do we learn
to trust?

Your Story

I love to hear poetry.
I love to read poetry,
   and I love to write.

I love
to feel, to sense
to teach with
depth and meaning.

For me,
I want to tell
   a story.

A chapter of
who I have been
who I am now
   and
who I will be.

I would love to help you
say who you are in words
   that are knowing.

Spiritual Arousal

Tell us your story
about who you are
   and who
you dream to be.

You already move
through life
with a natural blessing.

I love that,
how you move and flow,
   so smoothly.

Describe yourself,
your personal being,
in meaningful expression.

You will tell the world
your story
and be known

as a gifted poet.

Doubt

It only takes
a little uncertainty
so small that
I am hardly
aware of it
A doubt that
throws me off
changes my confidence

and I don't even know
it is in the room with me

I feel it in my body
but wonder
just what am I not sure about

What am I afraid of?

Is it you
or
is it really me?

Am I just doubting?
Why do I have to know?

Where is my trust?
Did I wish it away?

What Will That Do?

My fear

has come true

You are gone.

Is this forever?

If I let go of my fear

      What will that do?

Thoughts At Night

When I wake,

unexpected,
from the middle of sleep,
I am often uncertain,
more afraid, less courageous.

The night
seems to change
my thoughts.

I often fear
you may not be,
but only with my thoughts
in darkness.

The light of dawn
settles me,
calms my illusions,
as I grow again
in faith and confidence.

The morning has brought me back,
the world is awakening
and I with it.

Oh, how I love the breath of
a new day and
the arrival of first light.

Thank you, thank you.

I have returned.

Why Do We

Why do we
Share
You and Me?

Why do we Open up
Not Judge
Not React?

What do we Hear?
Why do we Listen?

    Is it Trust?

Again

... and then,

when we get there,

everything,

everything will change,

again.

... and then.

What Is It

What is it in your smile
that feels oh so good?

What is there in your laugh
that raises my energy?

What is that twinkle in your eye
that says let's have some real fun?

Why is it when I hear you singing along
 that I want to hear that song over and over
again?

Sometimes I pretend it's only for me
even though I know it is who you are.

What is it that makes me glow with pride
when you have a win or success?

What is it when you are gone
and I am wondering when you will return?

What is the unknown, unspoken bond?
Do I really need to label it or just love what it is.

Maybe it's beyond my understanding
but what it is, I feel.

You Are There

In the early morning darkness

I watched the peaceful glowing moon
    peak through the billowing clouds
that covered much of the sky

... and then it disappeared

Even though I know
it is still there
I couldn't see it

Now I want a tall ladder
to climb up to the heavens
and part the clouds

... to find you

I want to see you soon again
even though I know

you are there

The Star

Sometimes,
I shut down, turn off,
I lose interest.

And then,
on a clear night,
I noticed something,
a bright twinkling star.

I became aware of my breath
in the fresh cool
evening air.

Next I noticed
a group of people
coming together
to celebrate.

It all helped me remember
what life's all about,
what we are all about.

I loosen up
get turned on.
I get it
I get being alive.

Spiritual Arousal

I get
how we yearn
to connect.

I know
I have to do
more than talk.
I have to be.

It all comes together
when you join with me.

That Smile

That smile of yours
there it is again.
Oh my gosh,
    that smile.

It attracts me
It draws me closer
    pulls me in.

That starry-eyed smile
you have, is magic
    to my being.

I forget everything else
Where am I?
What was I going to do?
    Where was I?

Oh my gosh!
now I am lost
but you don't know

    as I just smile back.

Telling You

Your silence
toys with my fears.

I am so afraid
so unconfident.

Tell me who I am to you.

Tell me what you see,
how you feel.

Tell me about you
What are you doing?
Why do you work?

Who are your friends?
What do you believe in?

Please tell me who I am to you.

Now how do I tell you

I have the same silence.

Please Stay

Please stay with me.

I only say this in my thoughts
not wanting you to hear me beg
not wanting to feel weak and needy.

Please touch me,
in any way,
it changes my whole demeanor.

Please look at me
with those beautiful, engaging eyes
that warm me and melt me.

Please undress me
and wrap me into one
with you.

Oh please read my mind.

Somehow I can't talk

Please, please know
somehow just know how

I want you to stay.

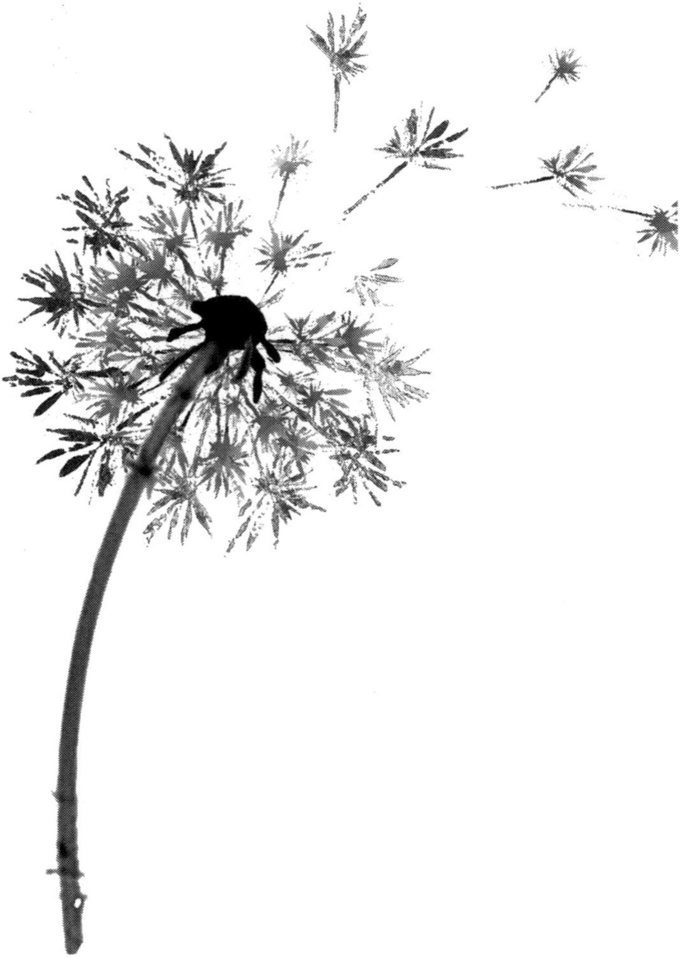

2
Whispers of Intimacy
Tuning in

Today's Intention: to be aware of the amazing benefits of silence

The Awareness of the Whispers of Intimacy

What will they be?

Chapter 2 embraces a deeper level of focus by listening, with more awareness, to our thoughts, beliefs, and inner self. It is about warming up our comfort levels, and the energy of connection with its natural intimacy vs our daily, habitual, repetitive thoughts of doubt and uncertainty.

An awareness of Connection, Communication, and Change with Inner Silence, Listening, and Letting Go as our focus.

> "Be quiet and Still.
> The Whispers are There,
> Are you listening?"

Listen

Listen

for
the Whispers of Intimacy.

How do they behave?

Be quiet.
Be still.

The whispers are there,

Are you listening?

They are searching for you.

Hands

Your hands
    hold me,
        I feel safe.

Your hands
    gently caress me,
        I feel calm.

Your hands
    help me,
        I feel grateful.

Your hands
    touch my face,
        I feel in love.

Your hands
    laced with mine,
        I feel connected.

Your fingers
    lightly touching,
        always letting me appreciate
            that you are there.

Both of us
 our hands
  telling each other

   all we need to know.

Knowing

The sense

of
feeling connected
to you,

knowing
you are there,

helps me

walk

on

water.

Invite

I had to learn

to let you inside my head,
to let you hear my thoughts.

I had to trust
that it would be safe,
that you would not turn away.

I did
and now
I want to invite you

deep
inside
my heart.

Between

The little things

    you are

in between what
    you say

I feel them

    they are love.

Silent Inspiration

One quiet morning,

I hope you write
    about "Beauty"

and what it says to you
    when it whispers

in the silence that
    you are sharing.

Without Words

Being still,

sensing you,
in the quiet moment
of Now.

Being with you
without words,

just sensing
your presence
blending
with mine,

stirs a feeling
like no other.

A sense of
courage,
of wonder,
of strength.

I feel it
just being
still.

The Thin Line

There is
a thin line
between life and death,
between pleasure and pain,
laughing and crying.

Show me the boundaries
of darkness and light,
night and dawn,
of friends and lovers,
of faith and fear.

Always among us
everywhere,
in everything,
this thin, thin line between

telling us,
quietly and powerfully,

appreciate

what is
Now.

With You

I want to feel

alone
with you,

isolated,

so we are
totally unaware
of everything except
each other.

And when we are there
to hold, that energy,

that power of you and me

for when
we are not.

Flow

I want to know you,

to feel
your poetry,
your story with words.

Not just words,
your story with words and feelings.

Your story with words, feelings, and flow,
so that your passion
connects
with my yearning.

Then,
then I can feel what you feel,
know who you are,

through your poetry,

your story that flows.

Because

I know–

you don't
have to say
a thing

I know–

because
of what
I feel

I know–

Birth

If you look and actually see,

if you are aware that I am here,

always, always, always

here.

Then,

when it feels right,
you will know.

Then,

we will connect,
stir our creativity,
and from there,

we actually may
give birth,
to an emerging future.

The Flame

The flame moves,

dances,
back and forth,
around,

smooth,
as a waltz.

I sway,
dancing with you,
feeling the grace,
the flow.

You

bring it all

Alive.

To Be

Make sure,

my friend,

that

To Be

proceeds

To Do.

The Search

How deep have you hidden

your passion?

Do you even know what
it is anymore?

Can you feel a small
piece of it,
your passion?

Let me help you
find it.

The search itself
is part of the answer.

When found,
this passion
will ignite a powerful energy
of who you really are.

And with your new
"inner glow"

there is a gift

a reward

for all to flavor
in the charity
of your delight.

Your Touch

Your touch

your soft and
gentle touch

wakes me
brings me back,

Your kiss

your soft
and gentle kiss

takes me
so far, far
away,

So Beautiful

You are so very beautiful,

oh how I can see it.
You are so warm and tender,
I can sense it, feel it.

You are so hot,
can I stand it?

You are so sensual
I glow,
I melt,
I smile.

My knees are weak,
yet I move.

No

I run

to connect
and be

with you.

Lonely Nights

For me,

a candle
will always be
my reminder,
my memory,

of having you
with me –

and feeling inside
a warm and
comfort smile.

Thank you,

my light
on lonely nights.

In My Life

In my life,

> I want to be a channel
> for all that is pure and good.

In my life,
> I want to promote the flow
> from desire to passion to all.

In my life,
> I want to connect with, expand
> intimacy and profound love.

In my life,
> I want all that is possible
> and more.

In my life,
> I want to turn up the volume
> on this powerful, sensual,
> creative energy.

For all of this,
> now and forever forward,
> I want you
> in my life.

The Same

Tonight

I am wondering

I am wondering if
right now

we are both looking at
the same night sky

the same stars
with their mystery
the same darkness.

Are we thinking
the same thoughts?

Dreaming
the same dreams?
Feeling
the same yearnings?

If so
I know
exactly
where you are.

Silent Whispers

I love
    how
        you
            share

the
    way
        you
            feel
by
  being
      still

without
      saying
           a word.

I love
    your
        unspoken
            thoughts
and
    your
        silent
            whispers.

Reminders

It is nighttime.

I am alone and thinking,

thinking
of the special moments
that we have had

reliving
some of them again.

The times we had a sense

a deeper knowing

about ourselves
about life.

I am thankful
that you are there

a breath of fresh air.

A Lover

You are

    A lover of compassion and people
A lover of places and adventures
    A lover of flowers and beauty
A lover of clothing and appearance
    A lover of family and support
A lover of giving and sharing
    A lover of learning and knowing
A lover of accepting and not knowing
    A lover of allowing and believing
A lover of listening and patience
    A lover of smiles and laughter
A lover of quiet and stillness
    A lover of health and vitality
A lover of the mysteries of spirituality
    A lover of plants, trees, and animals
A lover of appreciation and gratitude
    A lover of books and movies
A lover of flexibility and possibilities

You are
    a lover of life.

I Am

In the shade

    of you

I Am...

Always

When I think of you
when I remember

it's like a gentle whisper
that only I can hear

A whisper that reminds me
a whisper that lets me know

that your touch is with me

always.

Lilac

They say

that those
who connect and blend

with the exclusive fragrance
from the bloom
of the Lilac tree

have the gift of taking in
with each breath
this remarkable moment

Also knowing
that immediately
it will be gone
promptly replaced by another

One whiff
creates a memory
never repeated
exactly the same

The Lilac scent is
a suggestion
a whisper of beauty

that seals this moment
forever being part of

who you are.

You Will Smile

When the Great Divine

whispers
quietly

listen closely
and say
thank you.

Others will wonder
what it is you have

What is your secret?

You will know

and you

    will smile.

The Sound Of

I found myself
    standing there
        just listening

Listening
    to the sound
        of gently trickling water

It was so refreshing that
    I thought of you
        and smiled

Then I felt
    confident, comfortable
        and ready

All from the sound of
    moving water and

        thoughts of you.

The Listening Breath

You are already Breathing.

Now
Breathe Intentionally.

Focus on your inhale and exhale

Then Listen
for the
Whispers of Intimacy.

Stay quiet
Be still

Hear them
The Whispers are there

Are you still Breathing?

My Mind And Heart

I worry about what
I am thinking

Responding from my heart
I sense my kindness

In my mind I am impatient, often blaming
In my heart I am gentle, fun & loving

In my mind I wonder what others think of me
In my heart I sense my compassion for everyone

In my mind I kind of mess things up
In my heart I smile at what is

In my mind are knots of Fear
In my heart is boundless Love

The energy in my body
swings both ways

My mind is untrusting and afraid
My heart is caring with a flame

I often think more than I am Being
and wonder why.

Your Gifts

You know

that smile
of yours,
that inner twinkle,
it's enticing.

It leaves your lips
enters my body
and stays there
throughout my day

You radiate warmth
a magical pixie-dust
the true energy of life

I,
being the fortunate one,
get to inhale it all

as it becomes part of my
internal light.

Your gifts
are being exactly

who you are

right now.

The Sun And The Rain

This morning

There is rain.

This morning
I realized

I think of you each day
when the sun arises.

I remember your smile
the twinkle of your eye

the joy in your voice
the brightness of who you are.

Then, this morning
I realized

I also think of you
when it rains

Fresh, Refreshing
Ready for
the next growth.

In more and more ways
You are here

Lighting up life
Clearing the air

The Sun and The Rain

Reminder "To Be"

It is nighttime.

I am alone and thinking.

I am thinking
of all the things
for tomorrow's doing

The busyness, the intrusions,
the calls, the meetings.

I need reminders for my to-do's
and also for my to-be's.

What kind of person
do I want to be today
and each day forward?

What habits do I need to change?
What will remind me until
the newness is ingrained?

I want to be
a breath of fresh air
to everyone I meet.

Who or what will remind me
on those days
I am off and feeling down?

I think it will be you.

Each time you come to mind
I will take a calm breath and
remember who I am.

I am thankful
that you are there

being my breath of fresh air.

Both Of You

This candle before me

represents my light inside

As with you,
it is warm, glowing, mesmerizing
it is thoughtful, intuitive, comforting

I take you both inside me
you and my candle of light.

Both keeping me
from feeling alone

Now I am being held
connected to intimacy,
in a reflective glow

bonded in togetherness
with my light inside.

Who I Want To Be

You are the Source of
many moments
where the magic begins.

Until I met you and
your way of being,

I had stopped believing in me,

not knowing
I could do anything

You define my space
where I want to be
who I want to be.

Merci!

I Believe In

I think of you often

I dream of you dancing
> I identify with your beliefs

I resonate with your thoughts
> I write about your intimacy

I empathize with your struggles
> and I smile with your happy self

I gape at your attractiveness
> I flow with your good fortune

I often breathe you in
> and just be with that
> as it is.

And most of all

> I believe
> in you

A Beautiful Friendship

We trust, safely sharing

our learnings and experiences,
our intentions and appreciations,
our thank you's and our wonders.

The Beauty of sharing our deeper, inner soul,
supported by the faith of understanding,
our natural awareness, and curiosities.

Understanding, sharing our fears, our doubts,

our beliefs, and insights,
saves us from constant inner judgments and criticisms
while exploring life and it's mysteries.

These are the personalized gifts

of a

Beautiful friendship.

The Pultneyville Grill

I gaze out the window at the Pultneyville Grill
   pausing for a moment as I wait.

Aware of reflections on the still water below,
   mirrored images of green trees and blue sky.

It allows me to see clouds in motion
   while looking down, instead of up.

A passing small boat creates a ripple
   that causes my image to disappear.

A few moments later, things settle and
   I am back to my calming clouds.

Still water creates a natural mirror to us
   to view life from a different direction.

I think of you as I realize that
   you do the same for me.

A mirror to life

   from a different view.

Always Listening

I am always listening

being aware
tuned in
waiting to hear your voice.

The magic of your whispers
never leaves my thoughts,
always being there.

I am listening
to hear them
over and over again.

I am listening.

Sometimes it is my
only purpose.

I am listening
to memories and
I am searching for more.

Always In My Mind

When you make a visit
to my thoughts,
I smile.

I want to sing, to dance, to play.
I want to skip, to write
to dream and to yearn.

When you come to my mind
I also want to be still
quiet and peaceful

Not saying a word
not being distracted
just being with thoughts of you

When you come to my mind
I feel the energy of life
and that, I love

For me,
it is a treasure,
you are here.

When you come to my mind
I feel your presence
it is here now.

You are
always
in my mind.

Another Hello

When I first see you

my hello is more than greeting
It has a really big smile built in

My body feels an expectation
a sense of acceptance
and appreciation.

You are such a joy
to connect with
and share our previous moments.

If we are together for two minutes
or several hours
I don't want it to end.

But then, again
when parting time
quickly arrives

When we hug
telling each other,
"Be well."

I know how
we will feel
when we meet again

Another chance
And opportunity
to say hello

Along with that
big, ongoing smile

waiting in my heart.

A Wanted Kiss

I was alone
late at night

basking under the brilliance
of a sky full of stars.

Absolutely so beautiful
I wanted you to kiss me.

But...
you were not there
so I danced and twirled
looking up as the whole universe
spun around me.

I was dizzy
connecting with your imagined presence
and the riddle of the stars.

I wanted you to kiss me.

I love this amazing feeling
I want you here
to seal it in my memory
with the way
you know how.

Believe–Feel–Now

Drop all of your excuses,
all of your stories
and Believe

right NOW.

Feel the appreciation and gratitude in your body,
for the miracles that are happening NOW.

Know that you will soon become aware of them,
but that they are here NOW.

Believe it.

The impossible is already happening,
Believe it–Feel it–NOW.

You are ready.

Yes! You are.

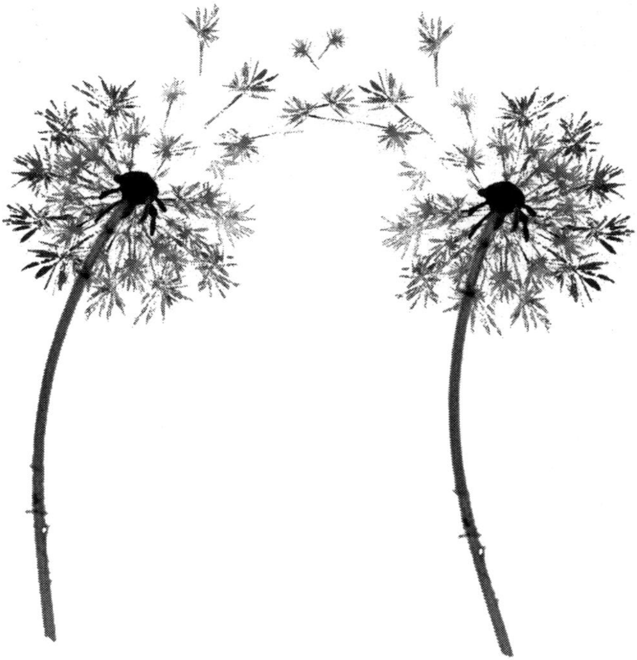

3

Arms of Oneness

Connection & Unity

Today's Intention: to increase awareness of the depth of connection to ourself, to others, and to our source of Spiritual Consciousness.

This chapter focuses on poetry and the beauty of connection.

Knowing the benefits of safe, comfortable, trusting relationships, starting with ourselves, followed by similar feelings with others is like a super power.

A logical understanding, as an example, is that we share the same air, the rays of energy of our common Sun, and the same water. We are created with the same core yet we focus on our smaller differences.

Think of this book of verses as a catalyst, and accelerator, to awaken your awareness of connection and its expanded creativity.

For each verse, see if you sense a deeper meaning after a moment of contemplation.

It's

It's Different

It's Peaceful

It's Inspiring

It's Fun

It's Now

It's Everything

    It's Awareness

Know This

Know this:
I think of you everyday
sometimes, every minute.

Know this:
having the spirit of you
with me

in my thoughts
in my senses
and in my dreams

gives me a strength beyond
what I could ever have
on my own.

Know this:
I appreciate you
how you are in the world
and having you here with me.

Know this:
I now have more
meaningful purpose
to my life.

Now, I know this
I finally recognize
what universal love
is all about.

I Can Fly

In my dreams,

I can fly,
not very fast,
not very high,
but I can fly.

I glide
faster than I run
and see things from
a different place,
a new view.

As I fly
I am looking for you
all over.

How present will I be,
to where you are,
gliding through
space and the all.

It is so very quiet
when I fly,
all sound seems to turn off,
so when I glide I can only
see and feel.

Now,
I sense you
everywhere

Wow!

Here And Now

We are here, now,

it is so powerful
how, together,
we grow.

Together in ways
we do not understand
and ways we would not
while alone.

Somehow we are guided
to be Here

Now,

in this time,
in this place.

Have we been here before?

It feels so right.

I know you feel it too.

An Offer

Here

    take my hand

and
step into

    tomorrow.

Connection

... then

can we connect?

Can we connect and
deeply feel,
 then
share that with
each other?

Can we have the gift
of connection,
that is us,
 together?

And when we do
when we have it,
can we make it,
about them,
with them

so that
they are
also
Us?

The Hunger

Why are we all
so hungry,
starving to be wanted,
to be known, as we are?

What do we need?
Nurturing?
Attention?
Support?
or
just to feel
the equalizing
connection of Oneness?

The bond that
we cannot explain
and do not have
words for.

Is this our deepest
desire,
to connect together,
as one,

and know it?

Circles

I am aware of circles and
smooth, round shapes.

Lines that go out and
return to where they started.

These circles and cycles
what are they telling me?

What are they whispering?

How do I follow them when
they always return
back to the beginning?

Will you help me?

If we hold each other's hands,
and form a circle with our arms,
what will we feel?

What is in our circle that
only you and I will know,
that only you and I can sense?

What do we have our arms around?
What can we not see
but can feel?

Together we may know,
or maybe,
Together, we will just be

in each other's arms.

Ray Justice

Big Three

Think - Happy

Speak - Truth

Feel - Love

Beyond

When I am with you,

physically or spiritually,

it is a curious mystery.

There is an instinctive knowing

beyond

what others label

Trust.

A Song

Could we write a song

you, me, and the stars?

I'll hum,
you start the words

Let's see

what color
they add.

Yeah!

I want to excite

your thoughts,

stir them with passion,

connect them intimately,

feel them come alive
and breathe
them in

Yeah!

We

We - You and Me

We - Spirit and Me

We - You, Me, Spirit

All One of us

Trust

You see,

I trust you

I trust you
     with me,

with the me
     I don't know yet.

And, you see

that

is
my

Deepest Trust.

This Moment

I feel the oneness,

the connection of it all,
being aware of each moment.

This is a creative and
purposeful life

It is being,

with you.

Ripples

Raindrops

touch
the surface
of a pond.

There is
movement,

Then ripples,

This

is how
it works.

We Are

Who are We?

We are Writers.
   We are Dreamers.
     We are Creators.

We are Here
   Stop and Visit.

Come and Be
   With Us,

     We are...

Alive

You

Help Me

Bring
The Future

Alive!

You And Me

I am here,
you are there.

We are different
in so many ways.

How will we be
when we are
both here
or
both there?

When our differences
are connected, merged,
what will we create,
from here
or there?

Let's bring it
together,

you and me.

The Quiet Spot

This,

this is the quiet spot.

The place
where I notice,
the sun,
the wind
the breath of life.

This is
the quiet spot,
where
I have nothing,

Nothing to do,
nothing I need.

Simply
being still
so that
once in a while
I connect

and
know it.

Ready

When the first snow falls,

I think of you,
the coming change.

What do you have in mind for me
this season, this time,

what shall we do?

When the first crocus blooms,
what will it be then?

Your changes, consistent and
always there.

I am ready.

I must let go of summer
and prepare for an autumn

I have not yet seen.

And then again,
as before,
as forever,

I have to,
I will,
be ready.

Remember

when we were together,

there was magic
in the air?

Remember
how it felt,
how it was?

Remember
the smiles,
the thoughts,
the touch,
the energy?

Remember
the awareness,
what we stirred
in each other?

I want more
 to remember.

And Then...
Something

Happened.

Night Sky

Many candles,
    many flames,
form a pattern
    that remind me
of the night sky,

the darkness,
    the stars, twinkling
with all their
    mystical wonder.

I want to show you
    the flames
and take you with me

into the night sky

into
    the wonder.

Beauty

Let's write

about

what is
beautiful,

in nature,

in life,

in us.

Let's Do It

Let's write

a story.

Who shall we be?

Where shall we go?

Let's do it

together.

As A Poem

I want to hear poetry.

I want to feel, to teach,
to sense, a poem.

I want to tell a story
of who I have been,
who I am and
who I will be.

I want to help you
say what you feel,
in words that flow,
that tell your story.

A tale about you
and who you are.

When you move smoothly,
glide and flow with grace,
I love that and…

I want to tell the world
your story

as a poem.

And Then The Stars Arrived

And then the stars arrived
    And then we were quiet
And then the evening ended
    And then we slept
And then the sun came up
    And then we awoke
And then we walked
    And then we stopped
And then we rested
    And then we ate
And then we talked
    And then we listened
And then we were still
    And then we thought
And then we believed
    And then we trusted
And then we smiled
    And then we felt grateful
And then we got it
    And then everything fell into place
And then we cried
    And then we laughed
And then someone showed up
    And then we felt inspired
And then we could breathe again
    And then it began

And then we connected
    And then we won
And then it ended
    And then we lost
And then we forgot
    And then we felt sad
And then we remembered
    And then we returned
And then we felt happy
    And then it changed again
And then we knew
    And then it came to us
We are one
    And then the stars arrived
And then...

Refreshing

All I have to do,
one simple thing.

I feel stronger,
confident,
more aware.

I smile
inside and out
and feel
shamelessly alive.

It's vigorous, refreshing,
like a whispering breeze
or
a cool drink of water.

A pause,
recharged, fresh
and ready.

All I have to do
 is remember you
being exactly

who you are.

Our World And You

Do you wish upon a star
  always wondering who you are?

Do you sense the twinkle within,
  knowing it will help you win?

Do you hold your heart in place,
  drawing in the love, with Grace?

Will you allow it all to flow,
  show the way with your powerful glow?

Are you ready to spread your light,
  as all those stars shining so bright?

Now, do you see
  all you have to do is be?

All that you are
  is already a star.

Rain

Rain makes the air
and my lungs
feel fresh.

The sun brightens my day
and makes my skin
feel warm and healthy.

Grass, the trees, flowers
are peaceful
quiet and still.

They keep me relaxed and connected.

Ice cream is my treat

You
        are my smile.

The Spark

Outside,

on a cold winter day,
a stranger approaches.

A smile is seen.

It travels,
through the eyes of the receiver,
searching deep inside,
until it finds the heart,

where it settles in,
as a small, yet powerful spark,

and warms up

the whole world.

Let It Shine

Good morn'n lovely
and be it a good one for you.

Today
feel the warmth and comfort
of the sunshine

and if it not be out

let it shine in your heart this day
and forever more.

Freedom

What I love

in you

creates

freedom

for me.

Your Laughter

You have rollicking laugh
in you
that I'd like to meet.

It's when you let it all go
not having thought
to look or sound neat.

Your laughter within
rolls on its own
as you feel fun, play, and freedom
with a silliness tone.

Laugh for me now
help me get going
Begin with a smile
'till the chuckle starts showing.

Then let it rip
loud and clear
hold nothing back
even bring a tear.

Let's howl together
with our internal toy
as we connect with each other
spreading wonderful joy.

So Far Away

Tonight seems so far away,
    slow in arriving.

Tomorrow seems close,
    almost here, so quickly.

The now of tonight
    the now of tomorrow

Reminding me of
    the gift of now.

Who You Are

I love who you are,
    the way you are in the world.

I love how you are so aware of others,
    so attentive, caring, and appreciative.

I love the way you think,
    your focus on detail.

I love your style of systematic doing,
    your follow through, your accuracy.

I love your very sincere interest in others,
    your desire to help, to assist.

I love your level of integrity,
    the way you are always fair and square.

I love your attitude of open mindedness,
    your curiosity, wonder, and willingness.

I love the energy that you consistently radiate,
    the smile, the graciousness, and kindness.

I know that you are a joy to many,
    as you vibrate the energy of happiness.

Reflecting Beauty

Today the river is quiet,
the stillness of the water,
creating a natural mirror.

The reflection from above,
being upside down,
is perfect and exact.

A replica of what
is actually there,
in this current moment.

Somehow, in a strange way,
I notice the image, the likeness
more than the actual.

The shapes, the colors
the sky, the trees
their Beauty grabbing my attention.

Pondering this view
my awareness increases
in a magical way.

I love and appreciate
the communications, messages
and the deeper essence of nature.

You have become my reminder
my mirror of reflection

for the Beauties of Life itself.

Balance (Julie's Poem)

As I sit
facing south
my left ear
to the ocean
with its alternating patterns
of surf and silence.

My right ear
to the west
the human sounds
doors, talking, autos

All at the same time
rhythm and stillness
energy and action.

The balance of it all.

You bring us back
to the warmth and the silence
to compassion and to writing
to caring and commitment
to uncertainty and confidence
to allowing and to focusing

By being who you are
we are more of who we can be.

You are balance and beyond.

A Lover's Stillness

Lovers don't have to talk,
there is a knowing
that doesn't need to be heard,
not even a single word.

Lovers know
by eye contact
by breathing
by touch and experience

They know Trust is not,
and can not be, spoken
It is known.
Trust is a Lovers Foundation.

True Lovers
can risk stepping outside
their self created box,
where they have drawn the line.

Once that intimate certainty
has bonded,
a portal opens,
new possibilities appear.

A Lovers Trust brings with it
the confidence and safety
to stretch, and to go,
where new adventure awaits.

A True Lover's Stillness
contains genuine heartfelt Trust,
and with it, an inner smile,
that is deep, silent, appreciation.

Wet Footprints (Lisa's poem)

Across the floor
Up the steps
Wet footprints
Outside
An ocean dip, a pool swim
A bike hike

Inside
A journal, A pen
A focused woman

Outside
Energy, in action
Next, Next, Next
Wet Wild Woman

Inside
coaching,
listening

Appreciating

Guiding

Now footprints
can remind us
to write
to listen
to add detail
to be confident
and...
if they happen to be like Lisa's
we will remember
it's ok to risk
and be a little wild

maybe, just maybe

leaving footprints of our own

My Reflection

Just as I see myself
while gazing
into a pool of still water.

I sense and feel
more of who I am
by my reflection
in your eyes.

You allow me
to feel like
a powerful hero
a talented artist
a passionate lover
a helpful servant
a witty comic
a personal inspiration
... and more.

Your eyes
alone
include me
completely

What else
could I need?

Lovers Almost

When we are together
we are almost like lovers.
The same energy
the excitement
the trusting
the sharing
the same direction.
You take away my troubles.
We have so much
without the entanglement.

When we are together
I feel your love
without being lovers.

What can we do for the world
with our love awareness?

Can we help others
to feel this too?

Me

I train my mind
    with stillness

I stir my thoughts
    with creativity

I refresh my lungs
    with the air of life
    and the Breath
    of Spirit

I sharpen my eyes
    with the
    Beauty and Wonder
    of all

I tone my hearing
    while listening
    for the silence
    between the sounds

I tame my ego
    by seeing myself
    in others

I warm my soul
    with awareness
    of connection

I lubricate my heart
    with hope, compassion,
    and possibilities

I move towards my dreams
    by taking a small step
      today

    and another
      tomorrow.

        Yes!

Dance, A Beautiful Thing

The sounds of the drum, the guitar.
We feel it in our body.
Vibration!

Our foot begins to tap,
we stand up,
shifting our weight just a little.

When our hips get involved
it is all over
there we are, bopping and grooving.

Our body rocking, shifting
in partner with the rhythm's
continuous repeating spirit.

We are totally tuned in
to the sounds and sensations
as they seduce our frame and inner being.

We forget our problems
our energy inflates
we are really in the now.

Spiritual Arousal

Then the music slows
the lights dim
we embrace our welcomed partner.

A union is instantly formed
we move, glide and float
like clouds across the wide blue yonder

Inspiring togetherness
dance establishes trust
followed by intimacy

Without speaking
We both feel and know that
dance is a beautiful thing.

The Image Maker

I am the Image Maker
    The creator of ideas and happiness

What is the image you desire?
    The life you really want.

Let's take your thoughts,
    The ones you repeat over and over.

Then let's erase most and change them
    into possibilities and fulfillment

Give me some thoughts and desires to work on.
    Don't confuse me with what
    you don't want.

I am forever with you,
    All you need to do is pause and listen.

I am always on call,
    free and available

Let's get started,
   are you ready?

Together,
   We make it happen.

Namaste

This morning I visited you
in my thoughts
as you slept.

Namaste

May you be sleeping in peace
wake in anticipation
and smile through your day.

I honor your quest
    for your own personal happiness
I honor the oneness we hold
    in each other.

I honor all levels of love and caring
    As we grow, change and adapt
I cherish our connections
    And appreciate our complimenting
differences.

Namaste

Pieces of you are with me always
    I honor that.

I honor who you are for you
      and... I honor who you are in me.

I honor your expression of freedom
      Of being who you are

When you are in your place of comfort
      I feel it
and I am in mine...

Namaste.

Arms Of Oneness

When I merge myself
    in you

when I wrap you
    in my arms

it is not only
    what I see or feel
        or how I touch

it is being
    with you

connected
    in a way

that has
    no words
        no description

We are joined
    in the Arms
        of Oneness

Closing Thoughts

As you finish reading or listening to a Spiritual Arousal poem, consider a few moments of silence in a quiet space. We often need silence for awareness of our deeper thoughts and whispers.

New insights may come to you as reviews; as you read, try this to enhance your own experience.

- Sit in silence or with soft music playing.
- Choose a random poem to read or listen to.
- Close your eyes and consciously, slowly breathe for a few moments after you have finished the poem.
- Open your eyes and immediately begin writing without hesitating to judge or analyze.
- Avoid critical thoughts; just begin.
- Continue writing for a few minutes allowing more profound whispers to come alive.

Many verses in this book refer to "You."

Who or what is the You in your thoughts today as you read? The same verse might create awareness of a different "You" tomorrow.

Another interesting experience is paying attention to each poem, one at a time.

Who or what you first think of after reading or listening. can become very enlightening.

Feel the connection. It's there and is another opportunity to write your new thoughts.

Ray Justice, poet, explorer of creativity & connection

Dedications

I am passionately thankful for my large, wonderful family, and trusting, helpful friends, that make my life a joy and a gift. In Appreciation, I dedicate this book to honor my mentors who are no longer with us.

They inspired me even after they passed. Their powerful lessons and stories changed my thinking and continue to motivate many of my current choices. I have immense gratitude for their shared experiences, personal connections, and inner gifts that I carry with me and pass on to others through their stories.

Introducing some of my inspiring confidence builders from my past who taught me to wonder and Be myself:

- **Dr. Mary Beetz**, who helped me when I did not know what to do next. Later on, we shared many deep what-ifs and enlightenments.
- **Mary LeSchander.** My High School French teacher who had confidence in me when I did not. She desperately tried to help me learn French. However, neither of us knew I had a hearing deficit and could not pronounce many of the words. She left me a surprising gift in her will.
- **Dr. Stan Dale.** When I was a kid, Stan's voice introduced the radio show I listened to every night—The Lone Ranger. He gave me a partial recording of his introduction, leading off with "This is for my buddy, Ray—With a cloud of dust and the speed of light …" A progressive and lovable man, Stan founded The Human Awareness Institute. (HAI)
- **Herb Agnes**, Commander of the Army National Guard, Rochester NY. I was quite young when he sent me to officer training school. I let him down after the first two-week session and decided not to proceed. I told him it was not my thing. He graciously excepted my choice. Later on, his wife told me he appreciated me and that I was very inspiring. I

found that intriguing because, at the time, I was still a young 20-year-old.
- **Leon Allen**, a Kodak colleague: I was an apprentice, in a mechanical engineering training program, when he offered to pay for my college. I did not take him up on it, mainly because I had no idea what to do. Again, I was 19. And to top it off, he didn't want me to pay him back.
- **Clarence Cooper**, my friend and golf partner. He knew me well and kept me from making a major business mistake. We spent many hours together, sharing our life stories as he taught me about segregation.
- **Lou Cocilova**. He left me this quote. "Only do the things, that only you can do." He reminded me to focus on the exact wording. He said he wanted to help me because I had helped him grow his business. All I did was ask him one question. "How would he dress and act if he was already a huge success." He did and he was.
- **Amanda Mack**, my friend and my Goddaughter, we shared common curiosities about spirituality, personal development and called each other with each new *aha*.
- **Mary Howard**, my friend who stayed with me for a summer while working to rebuild her life, basically from scratch. I admired her determination and watched her remarkable success in a few short years. I miss her chuckle.
- **Johnnie Justice**. My younger brother left us when he was seven and I was twelve. He left me with a lifelong sorrow and with an awareness to appreciate every moment while we are here. His passing, at such a young age, became a major factor in my own life purpose.
- **Bea Justice**, my mother, who taught me about being kind and helpful while appreciating my relationship with others. She lived to be over one hundred years old, walked at a younger person's pace, without a cane. At ninety-nine she began to slow down, but still didn't

need a cane, and she knew, by name, all fifty-seven of her extended family. She gave me my earliest inspiration and a lifetime of wisdom.
- **Willet Justice**, my Dad, who instilled my work ethic, built a business from scratch by working more than what seemed possible. That was every day, he felt free to make his own choices, and that gave him the drive to grow and accomplish.
- **Mary DeStephano**, my mother-in-law, a Master Home Chef, who taught me the power of fear and how it imprisons. Through my talks with her, I learned how to understand others by asking questions, examining their life experiences.
- **Ralph DeStephano Sr.**, my father-in-law who also built a business from scratch and taught us his way. Some good, some tough as I learned business basics and Entrepreneurship.
- **Helen Burke**, my Aunt. I spent many summer hours on their farm working and playing. It was a refreshing change of environment and even better with her lovable attitude. It was needed in my early teens dealing with a house fire, younger brother's death, being bullied, and a new school.
- And those whose paths I was fortunate to cross after studying their teachings; Wayne Dyer, John Denver, Leo Buscaglia, Dennis Weaver.

My Heart flows with appreciation.

Acknowledgments

Some of the people that have helped and inspired me along the way, in this case, especially with expressive writing and deeper expression.

Spiritual Arousal Cover and Graphics Creative Team

• **Jill Stolt** introduced the initial cover theme and internal graphics for Spiritual Arousal. A creative, compassionate hard worker, she develops amazing, artistic, entertaining programs with teens. **Wellventions.org**
• **Julie McKown**. My other hand with this book and many other projects, a gift to know and work with. Multi-talented with Virtual Production and Communications. She covers all the details with a responsive adaptable attitude, and is also a talented singer.
PocketSquare.info
• **Sheila Kennedy** got me started with early helpful guidance on book writing, where to begin. Easy to work with and has a helpful e-Magazine titled *Zebra Ink*.
TheZebraInk.com
• **Sandy Evenson**, my brilliant, hardworking compassionate partner, editor, and author of *The Woo Woo Way, Unblock Your Chakras and Transform Your Life*.
SandyEvenson.com
• **Patsy Balacchi** brought us together and added her own thoughts and creativity to end with a home run cover. She's an expert in graphic design blended with Feng Shui.
Zenotica.com
• **Christine Kretchmer**, official website designer and my favorite daughter, with an inquiring and inspiring attitude.
RayJustice.com
• **Evan Grip** is my always-willing Spanish translator, course arrangements technical admin and researcher.

- **Wendy Brabon**, a longtime friend and bright, detailed, storyteller. An expressive writer with a commonsense depth that I love. I was thrilled when she agreed to write a short Foreword for this book.

With Inspiration and influence from:

• **Dr. Brian Justice**, my younger brother always ready to encourage and share compassionate ideas.
• **Julie Colvin & Lisa Fugard**, Writers and workshop presenters with an open-minded, comfortable approach. My first professional writing retreat. They are well-versed and fun to be with. **WellnessWritingRetreats.com** & **Lisa Fugard.com**
• **Sara Wiseman** is a powerful intuition teacher, author, and entrepreneur who is also very likable. She keeps me tuned in Intuitively. **SaraWiseman.com**
• **Michele Pearce Cleaves** taught me a fun level of Intuition. **Common-Sense Intuition**
• **Marjorie Baker Price, RN** - Longtime friend and coach with writing and Intuition. Twenty-plus years ago, we co-authored a book, "Power Intuition," that Margie used in her workshops. **CenteringTools.com**
• **Christina Williams**. We worked together on my first much smaller poetic booklet and a successful live presentation. Chris is delightful, organized, and creative, with a wonderful mellow attitude.
• **Lucia Pinizotti**. My go-to friend when I need a new thought or a different question. She is a gift who knows how to dwell deeper. **MonopolyforChange.com**
• **Ralph DeStephano**, Entrepreneur, Developer. Thank you for your early insistence and constant nudging while getting me to write when I had absolutely no intention to do so.

- **Blair Hornbuckle**, Master Photographer, Techie, Philosopher, and friend, always ready with an unconventional deeper approach and a camera. **BlairHornbuckle.com**
- **Deb McGwin**, a Wonderful Photographer, and person. She helped me create greeting cards with several of my poems. **DebMcGwinPhotoAndDesign.com**
- **Dr. Seema Khaneja**, Author of *Physician Heal Thyself* and an ACIM (*A Course in Miracles*) coach. She is always ready with encouragement and peaceful, loving energy while following her heart. *CoachingForInnerPeace.com*
- **Alyce Adams**, RN, a longtime friend, passionate about life's natural and health aspects, focusing mainly on helping women. **KegelQueen.com**
- **Arthur Guariniello**, a longtime friend, and business partner of many years. When in our mid 30's he worked hard to convince me I had a unique and powerful presence. He showed me why I should be on stage teaching. (Which I did not do)
- **William Johnson**, the 64th Mayor of Rochester, NY. A close friend, supportive, and a master orator. He believes in me in a strongly encouraging way.
- **Rev. Lou Vasile,** my trusted, interesting, close friend of 40 years. We have shared many stories and philosophies and have more to go.
- My supportive and remarkable family: **Christine, Dan, Katherine, Sarah, Maria, Carl, Michele, Sky, Ivy, David, Jess, Olivia, John, Sheila, Nic, Julianne, Caitlin**, and **Sandy.**
- **Jerry Deluccio** and **Dave Coffey**, my friends and progressive partners in another business. They have idea after idea. EnchancedCareMD.com and ecPathways.com
- **Karen Orrico**, my trusted bookkeeper and friend of over

25 years. She retired, and I miss her every day.
- **Zarika Kohli**, and **Loie Ippolito**, current bookkeepers and organizers, are incredibly nice and trustworthy. I am grateful for their help in giving me time to develop and write.
- **Rahul Kohli**, my friend, is a master at business development and verbal communication. He is my number one go-to business friend. We meet and figure things out.
- **Holly Geoghegan**, a close friend of many years and a Pen Pal who got me writing before I knew what I could do. She is always on my creative idea list with inspiring thoughts. GolfMarketingInc.com

Others who have helped me with inspiration for this project:

- **Kelly Kralles , Rosa Montanaro, Clay Osborne, Jean Kase, and Sandy Baker**
- **Some of my favorite authors/ teachers**; Rumi, Hugh Prather, Richard Bach, Michael Singer, Thurmond Fleet, Brian Swimme, Wayne Dyer, Dr. Joe Dispenza, David Hawkins, Md, Phd, Tom Crum, Shakti Gawain, David Whyte, Louise Hay, Mark Nepo, Donna Eden, Brad Vanauken, Tony Robbins, Sark, Jose Silva, Jean Bennett, Barbra Sheer, James Redfield, Donald Russell Woodruff, and many, many more.
- And a large inspiring "X" representing the unknown values of those who I have not mentioned here. The X, used in math as an unknown part of an equation, represents their meaning and influence.

About the Author

A modern-day poet, philosopher, and entrepreneur, Ray Justice is an inspiring writer, intuitive mentor, and business and life coach. His unique style is a powerful source of Intimacy, Connection, Creativity, and Change. Ray sparks Curiosity by leading with a question which often leads to another question.

Ray J's business and personal coaching philosophies center around understanding the power and importance of connection. He teaches us to be more interested in our authentic selves. The deeper we know ourselves, the better we understand each other. An awareness of the voices inside our heads is a step toward understanding mental and emotional self-management.

Ray believes that we are all naturally creative human beings. Remaining peaceful, curious, and aware is a significant factor in what we create.

Known as a "Change Master," Ray uses unique, out-of-the-box problem-solving methods with an upbeat attitude of possibility thinking. He helps us tap into our Intuition and Creativity to find our particular, inspiring purpose.

Spiritual Arousal emphasizes Ray's spiritual and personal connection through writing and poetic verses, which follow a pattern of Attitude, Awareness, Curiosity, Intuition, Intimacy, Creativity, Willingness, & Intention.

Ray Justice has brought a whole new orientation into my thinking, and the way I interact with people. He is blessed with unique gifts and has been one of the most enriching experiences of my life.

Ray constantly thinks about ways to inspire people to think about the unfettered possibilities of living a life with a higher purpose. I am frequently amazed by the vivid explorations of his mind, and the ideas and inspiration that flows from them. His peaceful bearing, expressed in his poetry, is so refreshing in a turbulent world.

Raymond's Brain is one of the most fascinating, most creative, and curious, most inspiring places in the universe.

~ **William A. Johnson, Jr.**
CEO, Strategic Community Intervention LLC;
64th Mayor of Rochester, NY, 1994-2005

Ray Justice's thoughts are not restrictive or narrow and he understands change is not static. We have been friends for over 45 years. In that time, I have grown to appreciate Ray's remarkable ability to approach life calmly and creatively. His inner spirit is reflected in his poetry as he understands that it's about relationships, not rigidity.

"*One of the most creative, energetic, compassionate people I know, Ray has had a series of experiences that melt into his poetry, and that grows from his heart. He has a rare gift to put into words the sentiments of generations of the human race...He is also the most spiritual person I know. When I think of him my thoughts are of 'Happiness, Peace, and Thanks'.*"

~ **Rev. Lou Vasile**
Auburn NY

This book invites you to ignite your curiosity and your interest in poetry, yourself, others, and Spirituality.

Think, ponder, and write about your day— what you read, heard, or felt. Over time, you'll amaze yourself and become open to new opportunities. Your pen, pencil, or keyboard will take over and show you a creative, storytelling, or contemplative side you never knew was there.

Whenever you have an idea or a curiosity, write it down. Keep a small notepad in your pocket for quick notes or type on your phone.

Create a new habit of writing. You can even write about not wanting to write.

Writing daily for a few minutes will open your intuition and creativity. In a while, you'll amaze yourself. Read a verse from this book, then write about what comes up for you.

Find out more about Ray and his programs at
RayJustice.com

Dandelion: A healing herb, a symbol of happiness and delight.

Have you ever wondered why dandelions are said to carry our wishes to the heavens?

More than 5000 years ago, the Chinese began using the dandelion as a remedy and a tonic. Many other cultures have since used this unique plant to fight infection and as an essential staple of nutritious food. Because the dandelion opens in the morning and closes at night, it was also known as the "shepherd's clock." And since the shape of the dandelion changes with barometric pressure, some cultures have used it to predict the weather.

Pretty amazing, for a little weed.

The dandelion was considered so powerful and useful, that over the centuries it became regarded as magical. Monasteries grew it in their healing gardens, brides included it in their wedding bouquets for a happy marriage, and children and lovers around the world and throughout time have been blowing on dandelion seeds to make their wishes come true.

And what is a wish, after all? It is our intention, joined by our breath, and mobilized with an action in the physical world that has the power to bring a thought from a formless desire to manifest reality.

It's hard to imagine how this lovely plant - its yellow flower like the sun, its silver seed head like the moon, and its dancing, tumbling seeds like stars in the sky - could have become regarded with such disdain in our modern times.

Maybe it's because we have wandered too far away from our source and have become so enamored of intellectualism and technology that we have become blind to so many of the world's gifts—such as the usefulness, simplicity, and beauty of the dandelion.

Whether or not you believe in magic, the next time you come across a dandelion when it is at its final stage of life, and its fluffy white seed head is bobbing in the breeze, take it in your hand. Imagine what you desire. Inhale deeply and then blow out and send those seeds every which way into the air. You never know where they may land, but you can know this: each and every one of those tiny seeds—set free by your imagination and carried by your breath—has the potential to generate countless more dandelions and inspire countless more wishes.

That's something worth wondering about.

Testimonials About Ray Justice

Twenty years later, and I still go back to the bridge. What a wonderful tool.

~Mary Conlon, Retired Vice President, The Bank of Castile

Ray Justice is a creator and gifted thought leader. He belongs to that rare class of individuals who are open-minded and open-hearted. His passion for helping people and living life as an intimate moment has inspired within him an insatiable curiosity for understanding human nature. Focused on connecting the art of humanity to the personal challenges faced in life, he works as a guide to bring people through the process of self-awareness for a truer, richer life filled with new and satisfying possibilities.

Ray has but one mission here: to offer fun and creative guidance into the unknown, your unknown self.

Old Wisdom…New Possibility.

By the way, since we are on the topic, he has an incredible ability to inspire people.

~Christina Williams, Lifespan of Greater Rochester

Ray helped me through a lot of down moments, with his patience and great knowledge. That really supported me even far away. Thanks Ray! It's an honor to have you as my mentor.

~Lu, Program Coordinator Ideas Camp Education, Beijing, China

Ray Justice is a gentle, beautiful Soul. He reaches into our hearts and Souls and reminds us that there is great power and strength in softness and fearlessly models what vulnerable raw masculine power and tenderness look like and feel like. Ray truly embodies all of the qualities of a great healer… and leader. Ray is a Healer of Hearts.

~**Amy B. Martin Certified Energy Medicine Practitioner   AmyBMartin.com**

One of Ray Justice's many strengths is that he challenges you to rethink the conventional way of solving a problem, often helping you to see a new way to view or solve your situation. His real brilliance is getting you to truly understand your opinion or position and how others may perceive it. He lives by constantly learning new things with excitement, and curiosity.

~**Mike Masiello, A curious fan**

Ray Justice is an expert in thinking out of the box. He sees beyond the obvious and can take you to a better place through thought and exploration. He is different from most people because of this.

He is not afraid to test his limits and explore all possibilities in a kind and gentle way."

He touches so many lives and makes us all appreciate more of what we have in doing so. I will start practicing being happy and positive and appreciating what I have. No one's life is perfect, or even close to it, but we can choose to be happy! :)

~Suzanne Stansbury, Media Solutions, Schenectady, NY

Ray gets you thinking in a way that you have never before. He opens your mind & eyes to new possibilities and opportunities, that can make a huge difference in your thinking!

~Pam Kramer, Owner Pamela Kramer Stained Glass Studio

I wish I had just 10% of the energy, creativity, and insight that Ray Justice oozes. Ray has a way of instantly connecting, and helping others zero in on what is important in life. Even in a larger group, Ray has the uncanny ability to connect in a way that makes a difference. If Ray calls, make room in your calendar. You won't regret it!!!!

~Tom Merkel, Entrepreneur Chair Vistage group 49.

I have known Ray for over thirty years, and this friendship has been invaluable as I have moved through my various careers. Over several years, I invited Ray to address my entrepreneurship class at the university. Ray immediately connected with the students. He provided them with insightful business advice. But, more importantly, talked in depth about those intangible skills, talents, and personal characteristics necessary to be a successful entrepreneur.

Ray has a holistic approach to life's challenges that one does not normally find in business books.

~Bob Tobin Former Lecturer in Entrepreneurship
Simon Graduate School of Business
University of Rochester

I'm so excited about your poetry and sharing your work with friends. Ray is a sensitive, articulate, creative genius.

~Sandy Baker, New Perspectives/New Solutions

Ray is a calming force and adds a level of wisdom. He walks the talk as a mind, body, and spirit advocate and helps our team form a positive energy to ride the rough and good times.

~Jerry Deluccio, Author of Mzee, Musings about Life
CEO, Enhanced Care MD

I wonder how many people there are for whom you have left footprints, and their lives are never the same. Thank you for the many ways you give, inspire, and elevate.

~Lisa Hill DiFusco, President,
The LightHeart Institute (www.lightheart.com),
Rochester, New York

One of the most valuable assets in my life is time spent listening or conversing with this phenomenal teacher. This man has had a tremendous impact on my life; it's about the "feeling" I walk away with.

~Jeanne Apeland, Coach at Richard Robbins

Ray is masterful at combining phenomenal thinking with heartfelt compassion for others, providing a platform to undergo change, renewal, and introspection with relative safety. His joy and ability to seamlessly understand others while growing himself through partnerships has been a wonderful model for teaching others to lead while being led.

**~Clay Osborne, President
True Insights Consulting
Former Vice President Bausch & Lomb**

Ray's poems gently invite the reader to reconnect to that space of curiosity, wonder, and amazement that we all carry somewhere deep inside our hearts.

His words carry us out of the logical mind to a deeper intuitive knowing.

We are left feeling richly nourished with a sense of warmth and comfort.

~Sheema Khaneja
Author of, *Physician Heal Thyself*
CoachingforInnerPeace.com

Definitions

Definitions, as used in this book and by this author, are offered with the understanding that the same words have different meanings and uses.

Spiritual – Understanding and Feeling our Connection to all life, everyone, and everything. Having confidence and faith in the energy and vibrations of the universe.
A deeper intangible aspect with appreciation energies beyond our thinking minds.

Arousal – To waken, add energy, inspire, stir up, excite, turn on, the importance of being inspired about life, and having power, a vibration of aliveness.

Spiritual Arousal – Together, representing an awakening, inspiring energy for life and our deeper intuitive soulful meditative side of connection. A never-ending journey creating a wonderful life.

Verses – another word often referring to a poetic, rhythmic style of writing or speaking.

Connection – joining, relationships, friendships, Ties to all of life, Oneness, Unity.

Heart – used here to refer to an energy of affection and fondness, the core of our essence.

Soul – A deeper part of us that is Heart focused, the essence of our energy, who we are, the inner us.

Soulful – Full of Soul energy, of the beauty in life, a closeness enthusiasm for the Oneness of life.

Imagination – Creating in your mind, a mental image (of how you would like things to be)

Dandelions – A personal symbol of whispers, silent thoughts, dreams, desires, and intuition. As seen on the cover, Dandelions blend with the Stars of the Universe, a casual way to describe their inner connection here. Knowing yourself helps create connection and oneness.

Stars – Our Universe, a visual of the incredible creative vastness that we are all part of.

Wondering – The Chapter 1 Title - This refers to having a sense of Curiosity, Considering, Doubt, and Questioning.

Whispers of Intimacy – The Chapter 2 Title - In these writings, the term Whispers, represents the silent, intuitive thoughts, senses, and knowing that we have in our unspoken internal awareness. Whispers can be: Silent, Quiet, Unspoken, Soft, Calm. They are Sensed or Felt by our Intuition, our Universal Consciousness with a sense of an enlightened, informed knowing.

Intimacy – Closeness, Affection, Tenderness, Personal, Sensual, Safe, Trusting.

Intimate Connections – A feeling or energy of closeness, trust, and openness towards someone else, not necessarily involving sexuality.

What is it like to feel Aroused about life in general? Dr. Stan Dale, the founder of The Human Awareness Institute, taught, Intimacy as "Into me, you see." Being open, sensitive, and confident.

Arms of Oneness – The Chapter 3 Title - Unity, Wholeness, Together, Safe, Joining, Inclusion

> **Arms** – Coming Together, Protection, Cradled, Helping
> **Oneness** – Connection, Unity, Together, The Same, Inclusion.

Listening - our minds are hectic, often repeating the same things daily. Listening needs practice for most of us; it's about focusing and paying attention. If we are doing something else while listening, we aren't hearing. We have more distractions than ever, with most likely more to come.

Listening with a still, calm mind is compatible with Sensing Whispers.

Quieting our mind allows us to listen and be more aware of our inner intuitive messenger.

Personal Environment – the awareness and atmosphere of our surroundings.

Breathing and Stillness – Awareness in our body of a calmness, life force.

Intention – Our purpose of what is next. A personal expression of our next goal.

A Parting Message

Continue to enjoy your poetic journey.
May it brighten your world and inspire your appreciation for connections.

Thank you, and *adieu*!

Ray Justice
Rochester, NY

Let's Do It

Let's write
a story.

Who shall we be?
Where shall we go?

Let's do it
Together.

We are joined
in the
Arms of Oneness

-Ray Justice

Learn more about the author and his programs at:

RayJustice.com

Note to Myself

What if . . .
the Universe is trying to teach us the Importance of
our Connection,
to each other and to every living thing.

That if we live a lifestyle of helping others,

vs blaming, judging, or even ignoring,

we will embody a sense of
Appreciation and Love
that is Created by the Energy
of those we have helped.

That Energy may just be the power behind
the Magic of Creativity and

the Realism and Growth of Miracles.

Being Curious, Kind and Gentle
is a Strong Beginning.

~Ray Justice
Rochester, New York. December 2020

I wonder, who you are.

    I wonder, who I am.

        I wonder, who are we.

We are searching for a way
to connect
with what is the energy
inside our hearts.

Made in the USA
Middletown, DE
02 March 2024